DATE			

Advising
by Faculty

Dr. Howard C. Kramer is Associate Dean of Students for Counseling at Cornell University. Dr. Robert E. Gardner is Director of Advising and Counseling in the Division of Basic Studies at Cornell.

Advising
by Faculty

nea
National Education Association
Washington, D.C.

by Howard C. Kramer
Robert E. Gardner

Acknowledgments

The authors wish to express their appreciation to Lowell Balliner, Jr., whose insights helped frame early conceptualizations about the advising process. We particularly wish to thank Rita Gail MacAuslan, whose skill and dedication helped the manuscript become a reality.

Note

The opinions expressed in this publication should not be construed as representing the policy or position of the National Education Association. Materials published as part of the NEA Professional Studies Series are intended to be discussion documents for teachers who are concerned with specialized interests of the profession.

Library of Congress Cataloging in Publication Data

Kramer, Howard C
    Advising by faculty.

    (Professional studies)
    Includes bibliographical references.
    1. College teachers.   2. Teacher participation in
personnel service.   I. Gardner, Robert Eugene,
1944-   joint author. II. Title. III. Series.
LB2343.K7   378.1'94   76-54240
ISBN 0-8106-1610-6
ISBN 0-8106-1611-4 pbk.

PREFACE

This report is written to delineate the two levels of advising thought to operate in every advising relationship. More specifically, we have designed it to accomplish the following:

1. To provide a working definition of advising
2. To describe a theoretical framework for the process of advising
3. To show with model conversations the theory in practice
4. To provide procedures for advisor self-evaluation
5. To create a vehicle for discussion of those issues germane to advising.

This booklet is organized so that the experience of reading and thinking about the material becomes a model for structuring the advising relationship. We have attempted to design the booklet so that your relationship to us may be seen as roughly analogous to the relationship between your advisees and yourself. Throughout the text you will find comments enclosed in boxes. These observations represent our attempts to draw parallels between the process of reading this material and the process of advising or the advising relationship.

Time constraints may require you to use something other than a start-to-finish approach to this report. The following three sections may be read separately for a first reading: "The Process of Advising: How to Proceed," "Difficult Times: Tips and Problems," and "Models for Advising." Regardless of how you decide to use the booklet, our theme, persistently held to throughout the text is, Share it with your advisees!

H. C. K.

R. E. G.

> As you can see, the question of prominence at this point is, What do you want from this booklet? Later, you will find a useful application for a similar question about the advising relationship.

CONTENTS

INTRODUCTION

At one time or another, perhaps within the past week or so, everyone reading this booklet has gotten a note, memorandum, or phone call like the following:

Congratulations! You have been selected to advise freshmen in the College during the coming year. Your advisees have been requested to meet with you in your office on Monday, August 29, the first day of Orientation Week. Enclosed is a copy of the Orientation Week schedule, which you may wish to review before your advisees arrive. Should you have any questions, please don't hesitate to call.

Congratulations indeed! You have just become another victim of the dump-and-run philosophy of faculty advising. Your feelings? Anger, outrage—perhaps frustration. What to do? Call the department chairperson, of course. After all, faculty members have rights, too! But (alas) all you discover is that the chairperson is gone for the afternoon and that the memo is correct—you are indeed an advisor for this term, which, you suddenly realize, begins next week!

Now think about one of your advisees, who at this moment is enjoying the last week of vacation trying to determine what to bring to school and wondering if he will have a room to stay in after he arrives. He brightens, of course, when the mail brings a letter from "Everything University":

Dear Dave Student:

Welcome to Everything University. To help you in making out your course schedule and planning your studies, you have been carefully matched with a faculty advisor.

Your advisor is Prof. Friendly Stranger.

You should meet your advisor on Monday, August 29, at 3:00 p.m. in his office, B-248 Ivy Hall.

Have a good summer. We're looking forward to meeting you personally when you arrive for Orientation Week.

"Ah," says Dave. "What a relief to have a faculty advisor. Sure will be nice to know someone who can help me out. I wonder if he's very old? I hope not. He might even be famous. Jeepers, if he is, what will I say? I sure hope he doesn't make me take English!"

Unfortunately for Dave, from this moment on it's all downhill, for the more he thinks about his messianic advisor, the more he doubts, until, by the time Orientation Week rolls around and campus is a sudden reality, he is panicked at the thought that "The Advisor" won't be there and scared to death that this Nobel Prize winner with the Univac mind will be waiting, critical faculties fully poised. Hoping for the best, he fears the worst: "Welcome, David, I'm Goliath."

Whether your institution or department practices the dump-and-run philosophy is, in a sense, irrelevant, for faculty advising at this stage of the game is almost always the same thing: CONFUSION. Totally glorious, full-blown, uncontrolled, chaotic confusion. Telephones reveal no one who can be reached, the Orientation Week booklet doesn't have the answers, and the Campus Center is shut down for lunch! You are confused, your advisee is confused, your department chairperson is confused, and the coordinator of advising (what's his name again?) seems to have spawned the confusion. In a way, all this confusion is appropriate enough, for this is exactly the advising situation—confusion. *Fundamentally (or perhaps optimistically), advising is clearing up confusion.*

10

And that is what this booklet is about—clearing up confusion about advising. In that sense it mirrors the process of advising, and, to the extent that it clears up your confusion, it will have served as an advisor to you on the process of advising. What is clearing up confusion? It is defining, focusing, setting up the boundaries of the tasks of advising and observing them carefully, keeping agreed-upon standards and landmarks of advising well in sight. The function of the advisor is to clarify the situation, clear up the confusion.

> At this point we have moved from a loose, confused description of emotions and situations to a functional definition of advising. The literary vehicle demonstrates the advising process in both form and content. You know where we stand, what our basic boundaries are.

What does that mean in practical terms? What should you do? Let's return to our scenario. Confusion exists on two principal fronts: first, between you and the department chairperson or the administrator of the advising system (hereafter we shall use the term "manager" as equivalent to either); and second, between you and your advisees.

After you receive notification that you will be an advisor, sit down for a minute and let the juices flow. Get rid of your emotional reaction. Calling the manager with emotions aroused will almost certainly result in additional confusion (which is clearly proceeding in the opposite direction from where we want to go), so don't call immediately—unless you really intend to refuse to serve as an advisor.

When you have attained a steady state, scratch down—preferably point by point—on a piece of paper what you believe you are willing to provide as an advisor and what you believe the manager should provide. (We have written a sample list—p. 47—to stimulate your thinking, and we strongly urge you to take a peek at it before putting pencil to paper.) Then call the manager and articulate your desire to negotiate an informal but explicit "advising contract." State your view of what is required, ask in turn for his or her expectations, and, if necessary, arrange for a further meeting to reach agreement on disputed points. When you are satisfied with your contract, write a brief memo outlining your understanding and send it to the manager—for the record. Remember: your failure to be thorough at this point will only breed additional confusion during the remainder of your term.

What of your advisees? Do you need a contract with them? One purpose for having a contract with your advisees is similar to that for having the contract with the manager; it sets up the boundaries of your service. "O.K.," you say; "I'll give it a try, for, if nothing else, it sounds easy to do: just sit down, scratch out a checklist as I did for the manager (some of the items could even be the same!), put a space at the bottom for the student to sign (for the record!) and . . . ." No, that's not quite what we had in mind. Through the medium of this booklet we hope to suggest an alternative for your consideration.

Although it may seem right for advising to be managed so that your advisees accommodate themselves to your standards—that is, standards established by the advisor—reports of widespread failure of faculty advising efforts suggest that alternatives are needed. If your advising interchange is to remain a voluntary activity on the part of both your advisees and you, then models of advising need to be developed that facilitate the work of each party. One begins, we think, by striving to reduce the ambiguity about advising and the goals of advising, and to clarify the duties and responsibilities of your advisees and you.

> In successfully reaching agreement between both parties of what advising involves, you fulfill an advisor's function by clearing up debilitating confusion. You thereby set up boundaries within which you will provide service and eliminate some misunderstandings before they become disruptive.

The advantage of working on advising in this way is not difficult to see. It avoids the disappointment and bad feelings you have when your advisees come to see you depressed, because they have just received some bad news and you don't really want to talk about it. Conversely, it increases your pleasure if advisees do come to see you in this situation because you have previously indicated your willingness to extend your advising to these sorts of experiences.

Of course, it may mean that at the end of your first meeting your advisees may feel incompatible with you, and want a different advisor. Don't feel bad if that happens. It is certainly much better to know this on the first day than halfway through the year when both of you are dissatisfied with the arrangement. Bear in mind, too, that advisees and advisors come in all shapes, sizes, and colors: for every student who wants an advisor to be a close personal friend, there is another who prefers privacy.

In summary, if you accomplish the above—if you successfully negotiate these two contracts—you're off to a great start and we can promise that your advising problems will be few. But why the "if"? You're sure you could do it if you wanted to. Anyone could! Perhaps so, but, as with many tasks, it's harder than it looks. One difficulty is that few people are going to agree with you on the role of the advisor. Yet someone needs to produce agreement. Because no one is going to point a finger at the manager or the student for a job poorly done, the responsibility rests with you.

> You cannot hope to clear up the initial confusion unless you know exactly where you stand on advising, for the manager and the advisee will take advantage of—and later suffer from—your lack of clarity. If you don't know where you stand, the remainder of this text should serve to increase your awareness.

CONTROLLING SOURCES OF CONFUSION

Assumptions

One phenomenon that many of us at times would just as soon not acknowledge is that our actions are shaped by our assumptions. We respond to other people or situations in terms of what we expect to find rather than to what is there. Our assumptions about what others will think, say, or do often influence our behavior. The issue here, of course, is what assumptions, if any, we make about students, and what assumptions they make about us, as adults, professors, advisors. What sorts of truisms do we hold that may influence how we respond to and interact with youthful advisees? This is not to suggest that our assumptions are necessarily good or bad, but that we must be aware of the existence of an assumption *before* any corrective action may be taken. J. Bazelgette provides some examples of common assumptions about youth held by adult youth workers. Surely there are many others from your experience that could be added, but you will probably find some of yours here.

Assumptions about Youth[1]

1. Young people benefit most from interaction with those who are their own age, especially members of the opposite sex.
2. Young people are likely to be more helped to grow up by protecting them for as long as possible from undersirable contact with many aspects of the adult world.
3. Many young people need anonymity before they can be helped to reveal their real problems to adults and receive help from them.
4. Many young people are most helped to develop emotionally in informal situations in leisure-time activities, where the problems of authority are least apparent.
5. Young people are basically hostile to adults, and situations need therefore to be created in which this hostility can be avoided or at least played down.
6. The longer young people can be encouraged to stay mainly in institutions which are educational in their intention, the better they will be helped to settle down as adult members of society.
7. One of the problems for young people is that they are seen to be detached from the rest of society and appear to need help to develop new attachments to it.
8. The idealism of young people, springing from their clarity and freshness of vision and their flexibility in the face of change, should be made use of in attempting to change the nature of our modern society.

Our objective in identifying assumptions is to tease out the implications or consequences of maintaining such views, especially if closer examination shows them to be invalid. If, for instance, you hold Assumption[1] to be true, we might expect you to attempt to reduce time spent with advisees and to refer advisees to the more helpful students.

The bottom line (as they say) has to do with the assumptions you hold. We suggest that you take a few moments to respond to two questions:

1. What assumptions, beliefs, or notions about youth or college students, or advisees, do you hold?

2.   For each item listed, what are the possible consequences, positive or negative, of your assumption?

> The problems described here, in part, contitute the substance of matters to be resolved as you and your advisee draw up your advising contract. This contract, as any other, is a two-party effort. Thus, you must be aware of your position.

In a similar fashion you might dwell for a moment on assumptions about adults held by your advisees. Do your advisees view adults as persons to be sought out, consulted, or avoided? Do your advisees assume that adults desire to be told all relevant information or that adults will ask for information they need? Is it true that adults look for and enjoy opportunities to exert their authority over youth? The assumptions about adults held by your advisees are one major factor influencing the quality of the advising relationship.

Clearly, the assumptions you hold strongly influence the way you act. We have already drawn your attention to the way in which your assumptions about adolescents may influence the way you act as an advisor. Another way that assumptions influence the way you act or behave is through "roles"; that is, many people assume many different roles in the course of a day and act in a way that is consistent with their conception of the role required at any given moment.

Your Advisee

Your advisees have elected, presumably, to participate in a process called education. As students they expect that education will in some measure affect what they are, what they know, or what they can do. They recognize that the educational process will change them. For most of us, change is unsettling and anxiety producing. Ambivalence and unsureness in coping with educational tasks are sure to be present, and, for some students, coping is complicated by the task or process of moving from the role of young person to the role of adult.

Arthur W. Chickering discusses seven "tasks" of development that he feels occur during adolescence or early adulthood: developing competence, increasing awareness, clarifying purposes, becoming autonomous, understanding ourselves, understanding others, and developing integrity.[2]

About the time of entrance to college, most students experience a new phase of adolescence. In this phase, individuals have the opportunity to remake themselves in accordance with dispositions that may have been neglected or thwarted in their own family environments, and in accordance with the needs of the world they are each about to enter, a world often different from the one their parents confronted when they were at this stage in life.[3]

In that time of life where one is a young person-student-adult simultaneously, questions of appropriate role behavior are, at times, difficult to cope with. In Figure 1, the shaded area, where the roles of young person, student, and adult overlap, represents the point on a continuum of development from young person to adult that may prove to be most difficult for some of your advisees.

14

FIGURE 1

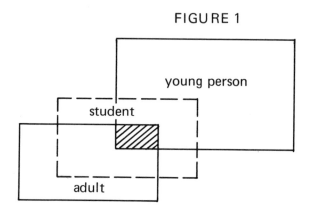

Learning to cope with this transition may be made more difficult because the student in many colleges and universities is surrounded by an array of peer role models. These role models are both numerous and readily accessible to the student although their appropriateness or quality are contested by some observers.

In contrast, personal contact with adult role models is frequently unavailable to many students. In many colleges only a minority of students become well acquainted with an adult role model that is available or accessible over time. Where such an adult role model is available, the student may try to imitate certain characteristics or traits of the model—in effect, to try on for size the mannerisms, styles of thinking, or other aspects of the adult model.

There is the need for adults in a college setting to be responsive to the student as an individual, to the student's particular strivings, competencies, and shortcomings. There is a need for encouragement, approval, and evaluation of the student's work. Learning and development take place at a deeper level wherever such responsiveness exists, as in the apprentice-master relationship of a student and professor working on a research project, particularly if this relationship is further deepened by the student's access to the professor personally, including home surroundings.[4] The advisor-advisee relationship is another such opportunity where the student may use an established institutional function, academic advising of students, to gain continuing access to a person who fills the role of adult.

Importance of the Adult Role Model

Bazalgette describes how young persons may go about the business of using close contact with an adult role model.[5] Youth are socialized or identify with the adult role and move toward taking a full adult role by modeling their behavior after others perceived to be in that role. Initially, the process of identification with the adult role by youth stems from interaction between adult-youth roles and moves toward adult-adult role interaction. Through exposure to a variety of persons filling the adult role, youth begin to acquire a repertoire of behaviors and perceptions that may be used to fashion their personal definition of self as adult.

Consequently, it is helpful for youth to have access to persons who fill the adult role. If the role of adult is juxtaposed to other roles of interest to the student—say, teacher, researcher, chemist, author, inventor—the process of transition to the adult role by the student would seem to be facilitated. The effect of exposure to adult models is to help young people understand realistically what will be entailed by their own adulthoods so that they can take steps to prepare themselves for it.[6] One significant contribution by faculty advisors is that of being available and accessible models of adults.

The role of advisor, as it is used here, is similar to the role of tutors in undergraduate education described by A. K. Rice: "If tutors can be found who, while taking a genuine interest in their students as developing human beings, do not avoid problems of the exercise of authority, they can provide adult models with whom the students can identify."[7]

From the advisee's viewpoint, the most helpful things you can do beyond the technical, informational aspects of advising are to try to understand his or her college experience, to clarify what is being experienced, to illuminate more fully the problem and the ideas or feelings that surround it—and to do this in a manner that exhibits a high degree of respect for the advisee.

The degree to which you feel comfortable about being accessible to the advisee, both physically and psychologically, is important. The advisee needs to know, to be reminded and assured, that talking with you about all manner of things is legitimate and acceptable. Therefore, it is important that you decide the level of commitment you wish to make before promoting these discussions between yourself and your advisees and to communicate this commitment to them.

The importance of conveying to advisees your willingness to engage in conversation and consultation is important. You've probably experienced many times the extreme reluctance of students to "take up your valuable time." Although such a consideration is not to be downgraded, if you are interested in offering your assistance in ways other than technical advising, you face a substantial barrier—students' fearing censure if they intrude on your time. To convey your willingness, you must do more than simply invite the advisee to drop by and chat. You must demonstrate that you are willing to take the time and are able to focus attention on the advisee and her or his reason for coming to see you. Arthur W. Chickering suggests that a helpful response by faculty has five necessary ingredients: listening, watching, feeling, inquiring, and respecting.[8] In dealing with your advisees, you must attend to the media, the message, and the sender.

The complex interaction of the tasks of achieving greater emotional security, defining adequate social and sexual roles, and developing autonomous competencies by your advisee demands that in your roles of advisor and adult you assume little, accept all available data as potentially significant, and proceed with judiciousness and humility.

Advisor and Role of Adult

One point we want to promote is that an advising relationship between a student advisee and a faculty advisor who incorporates the roles of advisor and adult is desirable and beneficial. Emphasis on maintaining the role of advisor and adult is needed because student advisees will, at various times, have need of access to a person who represents both roles. As advisors, faculty members provide specialized information and assistance relative to systematic academic progress. As adults, faculty advisors provide highly visible and easily accessible adult role models for adolescents dealing with the dependence-independence conflict associated with growing up.

In both roles, technical specialist and adult, you provide student advisees with continuing opportunities to explore and elect appropriate means of dealing with the authority of those persons in whom authority is invested. As technical specialists, faculty advisors are representatives or agents of the institution. Personal preferences of faculty not withstanding, faculty advisors are likely to be perceived as representatives of the institution. Even at a minimal level, the duties of the faculty advisor have to do with conveying, supervising, or enforcing policies of the institution. As the representative of the institution who informs, reminds, warns, or evaluates the advisees in relation to compliance with department, college, or university academic requirements, you are perceived by your advisee as an authority, and perhaps as an authoritarian one.

As an adult, you are also a visible and accessible representative of something that may be desired, feared, or reviled by your advisee, a developing adolescent. At times you may become a repository for the advisee of many of the projections, hopes, fears, and other emotions associated with the struggle over feelings of dependence-independence. The perception held by at least some adolescents that adults have solved such dilemmas and no longer experience concern over these issues may result in the conclusion that even in this area adults are authorities. Your role of adult made accessible by the advising relationship may mean you need to examine an issue of some importance to your advisee. That issue is, How do I, a young person, achieve the status of adult? What kind of adult do I wish to become? What characteristics do I, as an adult, wish to emulate? Increase? Eliminate? In short, how does one go about becoming adult?

Current Role Dimensions

Let us assume that some of your advisees will perceive their faculty advisor as one model of adulthood. What characteristics of adulthood do your advisees perceive you as emulating? Do they perceive you as an adult who is sensitive, realistic, quick-tempered, anxious, open-minded? Do they perceive you as an adult who handles stress in a particular manner? Uses a specific approach to solving problems? Is able to give and receive affection in certain ways? Do advisees view your manner of being an adult as particularly helpful, productive, or satisfying? In short, what kind of adult role model are you?

One of the pleasing and frustrating consequences of your advising duties is that some advisees will choose, and use, you as one adult role model. Independent of your intent to serve as a model of an adult or your image of yourself as an ideal or less-than-ideal model, advisees will compare their own image of adulthood with the model you provide.

What, then, are your views of the advantageous or unattractive means by which you deal with daily existence? What part of your style qualifies you to serve as a model for others? Are there approaches and methods of living you wish to share and discuss with your advisees? In summary, as a model of an adult, what do you have to offer?

Your response to these and other questions about your willingness and competency to discuss issues such as, What does it mean to be an adult?, provide a framework for the decisions you will make about how to conduct yourself in the advising relationship. This decision, distinctively yours, is one factor that will determine the nature of the resource you offer as an advisor.

ADVISING: WHAT'S GOING ON HERE ANYWAY?

Roles

You may have heard frequently expressions, such as, "In your role as an advisor" or "The role of the advisor is to. . . ." These expressions probably seemed perfectly sensible at the time. Actually, such expressions are nonsensical, for, in fact, the hallmark of an advisor is the adoption of a variety of roles, sometimes several different ones concurrently, yet rarely being consciously aware of any role in particular. Advisors adopt different roles so frequently that one can question whether an advisor ever acts strictly as an advisor.

An illustration may be helpful. Assume the first round of examinations is nearing completion. A student (David) comes to see you, a slip in hand, seeking to drop a course, or so you believe, since you see the slip. Having dealt with other students who wish to drop courses, you suspect he may be failing this particular course. Without pause, you begin to act in a role.

You may say, "Hello, I see you want to drop a course," and act the role of judge, prosecutor, or hostile witness.

You may say, "Hello, I see you want to drop a course. The math exam must have been pretty bad," and act the role of skeptical professor.

You may say, "Hello, what's on your mind?" and act the role of innocence.

Or you may say, "Hello, David, please sit down," and act the role of adult.

Assuming your advisee responds that he would like to talk with you about dropping a course, you may develop additional roles.

You could say, "You do have a heavy course load, it may be a good idea to drop a course," and act the role of student advocate.

You could say, "If you want to drop, that's good enough for me," and act the role of rubber stamp.

You might say, "Are you having trouble mastering the material?" and act the role of expert or master of a discipline.

You may say, "Are you having trouble with studying efficiently?" and act the role of teacher.

You could say, "It is the policy of the College that all students carry a five-course load," and act the role of authority.

Or you could say, "Why do you want to drop a course?" and act the role of facilitator.

There are, of course, many other possibilities. But regardless of specific developments in the interaction, sooner or later you may assume many of the roles described above. Consequently, you may as well face the fact that advisors are judges, skeptical professors, rubber stamps, experts, etc. You, at times, are all of these things.

Moreover, you are many of these things whether or not you approve of such behavior. By virtue of your age, you will be ascribed the role of adult. By virtue of your position, you have achieved the role of expert. By reason of your signing slips, you are an authority. No matter how tireless the effort, you can't alter many of these roles. Roles are "laid on you" and you live with the consequences.

Perhaps another example will help. In a recent advisors' meeting, a certain advisor asked if she had the authority to refuse to allow a student to drop a course. Other advisors expressed their opinion, and almost to a person their response was no: the decision belonged to the student. If the advisee wanted to drop the course after hearing all the advisor had to say, these advisors agreed they would go ahead and sign the slip.

In actual fact, this response by advisors represents perpetuation of a myth. The advisors, though aware of college policy regarding advisor responsibility, did not want this authority. They would have liked to believe they did not have such power, perhaps because it makes advising more difficult by providing conflict in roles. In reality, you not only have such power, you carry the responsibility for the decision. Authority is given you by your college. Since you cannot refuse such authority, you may deal with it through a mechanism that allows you to escape confronting this uncomfortable fact. Nevertheless, your authority is still there, and it is a role you did not elect.

The point is, you rarely elect roles. Roles are assigned to you by advisees, department chairpersons, administrators, or faculty legislation. Since you cannot rid yourself of them, the best you can hope to do is to recognize and use your roles in an appropriate way. What is an appropriate way? One which minimizes confusion. Remember, good advising produces clarity, and the effective advisor is clear about the role being played at a particular time.

Within each of your many other roles the expectations you hold for yourself, or those which are held of you by others, may be in conflict with expectations associated with you as an advisor. For instance, your advisee's expectations of your availability as advisor in meeting his or her needs may clash with the time demands of your roles as researcher, instructor, writer, parent, etc. In like manner, the different expectations within the role of advisor may not be in harmony. For example, the expectation of advisor as agent of the institution, or interpreter of college policy, may clash with the expectation of advisor as friend or confidant. Confusion results when your advisee does not understand your role, or when you assume more than one role at a time.

A first step in alleviating confusion is to increase your awareness of roles and your ability to recognize commonly assumed roles. The following definitions may prove helpful:

1. Adult—one who combines age and experience to cope successfully with life; grown; mature.
2. Expert—one whose training, achievement and position signify mastery of a subject matter area; specialist.
3. Teacher—one who is charged by an institution with transmission of skills, knowledge, or information to others; educator; instructor; tutor.
4. Researcher—one who has past or present involvement with functions and activities that may be so labeled; investigator; explorer.
5. Friend—one with whom one has an emotional and personal attachment (affection); companion; confidant; comrade; associate; companion.
6. Judge—one who by virtue of special skills, training, or position is afforded the activity of evaluating or assessing; arbiter; judicator; critic.
7. Authority—one who has prestige and/or power and/or is accorded sanction by an institution to give directions and have them carried out; official.
8. Rubber Stamp—one who confirms, agrees, or affirms the position of another.
9. Lecturer—one who is charged with the responsibility of providing systematic instruction in a body of knowledge using a formal verbal presentation.
10. Citizen, parent—one whose residence in a country or acquisition of position of parenthood are accorded role descriptions.

FIGURE 2

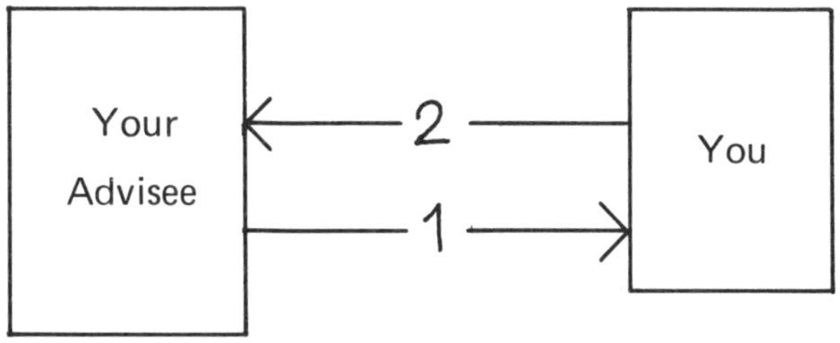

Awareness of the possible roles you play may now be tempered by awareness and understanding of your advisees.

If advising is successfully clearing up the elements of confusion, we need some way of modeling the advising interaction so that we can identify the sources of confusion, understand them, and postulate actions that would help in rectifying the situation. We can begin by asking what happens when your advisee steps into your office to ask you a question.

Normally, you would undoubtedly answer the question. Let's represent that by putting down two boxes, one for you and one for your advisee, with arrows in between to symbolize the communication. This basis interaction, then, is two boxes with two arrows. See Figure 2.

Perhaps we can be more concrete. Suppose your advisee steps in and says, "Hello. I'd like to talk to you about dropping a course." Now, you could respond in many ways. You could say, "I'm sorry, but the deadline for dropping courses is past, you'll have to make out a petition." Or you could say, "It's too early in the term to know how you are doing, why don't we wait a while?" Or you could say, "In general, I think it a bad idea for students to drop a course, because they waste the time they create." You might say, "Why do you want to drop a course?" Or you might say a great many other things.

The point we wish to make is simple: you could respond in a variety of ways, but each of these different responses represents a selection of a role you deem appropriate for yourself in answering the question. For example, if you respond with a deadline quotation as in the situation above, you are acting in the role of institutional authority. If you respond in one of the other ways, you act out a different role. When you think about this for a moment, you will realize this variety of roles you play as an advisor is almost endless—you may have played many of them today. This has important implications for understanding advising, because it means that you are not a box as we described you above; rather, you are a big box containing many little areas, each of which represents an advising role. You probably route incoming messages to one of the role boxes, and send outgoing messages from a role box somewhat in the way that we have indicated in Figure 3.

For most of us, it is not hard to see that we respond in different roles, because these roles are imposed on us and reinforced by time and society and we use them all the time; it is easy to know that we are professors, teachers, parents, spouses, etc., and to act differently in different situations. Experience teaches us what role is appropriate for a given situation. It is more difficult for most of us to recognize that others have a variety of roles to play, particularly as the individual is farther away from us. While we may readily identify and appreciate the roles of professors or spouses, we have more difficulty identifying those of doctor, executive, garbage collectors, or whatever. Because many of us are relatively distant (in time) from student status, we have difficulty in appreciating the fact that students, our advisees, have as many roles as we do. As a result, we sometimes fall into the trap of thinking that our advisees are single boxes, even when we know that we are not. Yet when we think about it, we know that advisees are very similar to ourselves—which suggests that we need to alter our model, as in Figure 4.

Utilizing this more complex model, we can now understand more clearly what happens when an advisee comes to your office to initiate an interaction. Generally, your advisee will express a need (often in the form of a question) that originates in one of the role boxes but surfaces from the larger box. Once a question is asked or a need expressed the ball is in your court. Usually, one of three things happens:

1. If the advisor forgets the role boxes, the advisee is treated as a single box, and the advisor answers from any role box.
2. The advisor may guess which role box the question is coming from, and answer with the most appropriate role available.
3. The advisor may ask for a clarification before answering from any of his or her role boxes.

If we analyze Situation 1, we can diagram what happens as in Figure 5, with the numbered arrows representing the order of response.

In essence, the result of the interaction is confusion on the part of the advisee. As the advisee generates repeated questions trying to get through to a particular role box, the one that corresponds to the role that he or she is using as the source of the question, and you respond with the wrong role or respond with a role directed to the wrong box, the confusion continues. If neither of you recognizes the problem, the arrows in our diagram multiply endlessly. Permit a concrete example to clarify things.

Again let us assume that your advisee comes in saying he or she wishes to drop a course, in essence sending a message from his or her student role. You respond that the deadline has passed, calling on your "authority role." Your advisee passes that on to an "adolescent" role rather than a student role, because the former is where authority is a question. The advisee then says, "I don't see why I can't drop a course now," thus aiming at your authority role, but, not recognizing this, you route the question to your advocate box and reply that those are the rules of the administration or college or whatever, and that even though you want to help, you can't. And so it goes. In hit-or-miss fashion, numerous roles are played by both parties, as they respond back and forth from their repertoire. Should both parties wish to do so, inappropriate role playing could go on until someone gives up or you both respond from appropriate boxes. Naturally, if you don't recognize what is happening, you simply take your chances getting to the right role.

Let's analyze Situation 2. That is, suppose you are somewhat aware of the fact that advisees have roles, too, so you make a guess when a question arises. If you make the right guess, all goes well. But if you make the wrong guess, you quickly get into Situation 1, with the slight advantage that instead of playing willy-nilly, you can gradually home in by narrowing down various possibilities. Essentially, you learn to make educated guesses. And it must be said that sometimes this is the best approach. Sometimes your advisee doesn't really know what

21

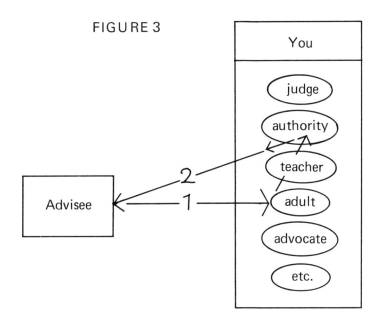

FIGURE 3

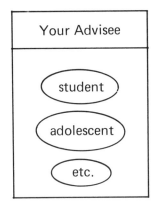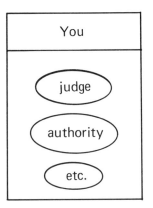

FIGURE 4

questions to ask. Your advisee may ask one question and find that your answer leads to another area, so that your attempts to guess at roles and respond appropriately will get the job done and done well. Advisors with enough experience can usually recognize roles and hidden questions and use this method to great advantage.

In Situation 3, when a student asks a question, you make your first move an attempt at clarification. You might say, for example, "I am not sure what you are asking of me. Are you asking if I have the authority to let you drop a course? Are you asking if I will let you drop any course? Are you asking if I will let you drop a course for good reason? What are you asking me?" Your advisee can then attempt to clarify the question, and you can respond accordingly. We can diagram the interchange as in Figure 6.

It is possible that your response, even if it comes from the right role and is directed to the right role, may raise other questions. You should be ready for this, and in fact you may want to encourage questions by explicitly recognizing that other little boxes are there. Thus, you may want to say, "I can see that I have answered your original questions, but I think my answer may have raised other issues." Or you could even take a stab at the other issues by noting, "I have answered your question as an authority speaking for the college, but I feel that as your advocate we need to discuss other aspects of your question."

This brings up a further advantage of our diagramming advising interchanges. Now you can see that not only are there role boxes, but that these are interconnected rather than independent. You can rarely respond from one of the role boxes without affecting or involving the others. That is, if you respond to a question only from your authority role, you also say that the other roles are irrelevant. If you say that one role is only partially relevant, then you also say that other roles must be brought into play. As an advisor, you can rarely respond with one role alone, because an advisor is, by consensus, more than one role. In fact, one convenient way of viewing yourself as an advisor is by seeing yourself as a box of roles so closely interconnected that your function is to include many (not just one) in any interaction. The differences between this advising state and confusion are critical, for it is the advisor who must be sure to include and discuss the different aspects in such a way that they do not become jumbled together. Clarity comes through identifying and communicating "where you are coming from."

We are now in a position to think about what advising is and how it is facilitated. Advising is (1) clarifying needs through the recognition and identification of advisee and advisor roles and (2) responding to or meeting needs arising from the role acted by the advisee with one appropriate or parallel for the advisor. Advising is greatly enhanced or facilitated by an advisor's awareness of the interconnectedness of the many roles played and willingness to incorporate these roles in the discussion one at a time rather than mixing them together.

23

FIGURE 5

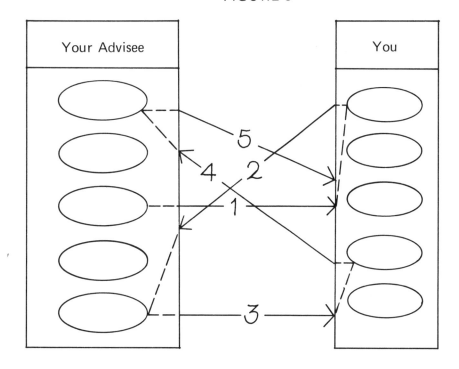

FIGURE 6

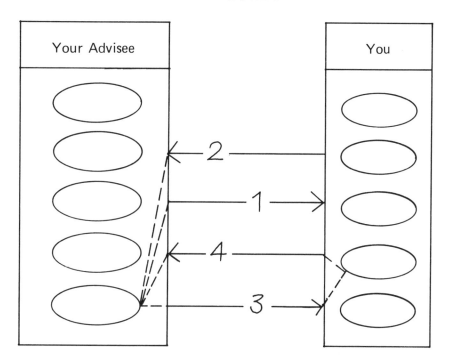

THE PROCESS OF ADVISING: HOW TO PROCEED

Academic advising is a continuing process with sporadic contact between two parties. The process may be described by an anology: the student advisee is climbing a ladder called education, maturation, or achievement. At various points on the ladder are landings—places to rest, to review progress, and to plan for subsequent efforts. (These landings, by the way, will probably be located at different places on the ladder according to each climber's needs.) The advisor's responsibility is to be available at each of the landings to help the climber review and learn from past efforts and to plan for what lies ahead.

The advisor's actions and the needs of the advisee may be seen as occurring on two levels. One level, we'll call it Level A advising, occurs when the advisee has need of technical assistance, information about procedures for dropping a lab, placement in an advanced section, how to preregister, and so on. The advisor, in the role of advisor, provides technical assistance in the form of policy interpretation, information, checking for errors, or other assistance to the advisee.

The second level of advising, call it Level B advising, occurs when the advisee is experiencing difficulty in understanding, interpreting, and differentiating the roles of youth, student, and adult. Here, the advisee experiences the "pangs of maturing," is perhaps unsure of his or her own self, goals, and abilities, or is battling with extreme feelings of dependence or independence relative to the institution, department, or specific individuals, including at times the faculty advisor. The needs of the advisee at this level of advising are not a matter of content or of specific information, but a process—an acceptance of feeling, an understanding of self in the situation, a definition of prior or future tasks, or a resolution of conflicts about authority. The advisor, in the role of adult, is one accessible role model of adulthood available to the advisee. Through interaction with the advisor, the student advisee is able to observe, identify with, copy from, or rely on a sympathetic, and hopefully empathic, adult. Level B advising provides the advisee with opportunities to work through difficulties associated with being an adolescent as well as being a student by means of an interaction with a knowledgeable and understanding adult. Most of you have probably experienced situations where the technical, informational aspects of advising (Level A) were completed but the student was reluctant to leave and may have made several attempts to chat with you. The need unexpressed, and in many cases unfilled, is for Level B advising—to talk with an adult about all manner of things.

Association with an adult encourages a student to work out conflicting feelings about adults who may be perceived as holding positions of authority and control. In the advising relationship, this perception is both real and subject to exploration. The advisor does have some measure of authority, however minute it may be, over the student. In the advising setting, however, the need for such authority, or the advisee's reaction to authority or figures that represent authority, may be explored and, within that relationship, possibly changed.

Another value of Level B advising is suggested by Stanley H. King's observation that the developmental process appears to be more successful when students have an early identification with parents or other adults.[9] These relationships provide a showplace for attitudes, values, or ways of coping that the student may then adapt to his or her own personality. The relationship between advisee and advisor offers a similar opportunity.

Figure 7 illustrates the two levels or parts of the advising process. For many problems, you may find that both levels of assistance are required. Or, in other words, you may have to go around again for some problems. For instance, a

FIGURE 7

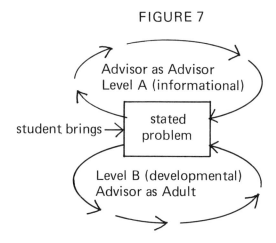

problem about academic requirements may depend upon communication with the advisee regarding requirement content (Level A–informational). Furthermore, advisors may also find themselves talking with students about the nature, rationale, and consequences of academic requirements, or about what is accomplished and not accomplished by such requirements. This latter discussion may be seen as Level B (developmental) advising, where the advisor in the role of adult assists the advisee in dealing with (accepting, understanding) the authority of the institution to create such requirements.

General Goals for the Advisor

Although it is usually risky to tell others what they should do, we think it may be appropriate to label some things that you may already find yourself doing. It seems to us that beyond the complex activity of information exchange, advising is composed of activities that may be fitted into one or more of the following categories:

1. Assuming responsibility
2. Defining and stating goals and objectives
3. Exploring alternatives and optional strategies to achieve desired ends
4. Making choices or reaching decisions
5. Coping with authority.

This list is based on an assumption that each advisee is engaged in the task of gaining some degree of mastery and control over the immediate and, to some extent, future environment. The process of education, whether gained in the classroom or outside a formal course curriculum, involves the task of receiving inputs and of producing outputs. The outputs may be increased understandings, competencies, skills, information, or other learning outcomes that enable the advisee to understand and control the environment.

In both Level A and Level B advising, the advisor acts to assist the advisee in planning, mastering, and understanding the formal and informal educational opportunities that surround the advisee. To go back to the example of the advisee climbing a ladder, each rung of the ladder, or set of rungs if there are multiple ladders, represents a new input to the advisee. As the advisee encounters a progression of learning experiences, the need for opportunities to reach a landing where he or she may review progress and plan for future activity may be changed, but it is not elimiated. Both Level A and Level B advising will, we think, be directed toward assisting advisees with combinations of the five general categories of activity mentioned above. Whether the problem is course planning, career exploration, or concerns about appropriate role behavior for the developing person, in most instances the advising interaction concerns itself with the advisee dealing with quesitons about responsibility, goals, alternatives, decision making, or authority exercised by others.

The Advising Contract

Advising is a series of activities undertaken by two principals, advisor and advisee, to accomplish the advisee's, and to some extent the institution's, goals for progress through a complex learning experience. The advisor is the institutional representative charged with aiding the advisee in formulating those goals and in making reasonable or systematic progress to achieve them. In a sense, the advisor is both an agent of the institution to ensure that the advisee achieves minimal standards and an agent of the advisee in achieving advisee standards.

In order for the advisor to carry out the primary task of acting in the best interests of the advisee, both parties must be clear about what is involved. For this we have proposed negotiation of an advising contract. An early portion of the advising interaction might best consist of discussion between advisor and advisee about the nature of advising: What does the advisee expect of the advisor? What is the advisor willing to provide? What is needed by the advisee? What are the special skills (or limitations) of the advisor? What is the principal task to be accomplished? How is progress in advising to be measured? How will difficulties that arise be handled? The questions to be explored, the things about the other person to be learned, the terms to be defined—all seem unending. Yet it is this beginning, this knowing, understanding, and accepting of the task to be done that make up the advising process.

From this pool of mutual understanding flows the advising contract. A shared definition of what is to be accomplished, the principal duties of each party, and the procedures to be used to monitor, evaluate, or change that relationship make up the advising contract. Since each party has personal needs as well as resources, the contract represents a compromise acceptable to both.

The advising contract, pact, package, or what could even be termed *bag*, even though it may be less than a formal written document, spells out the duties of the advisor and advisee in their joint effort to reach shared goals. The contract may be seen as defining the boundaries of those specific activities to be pursued by each party. The terms of the contract specify activities that are acceptable as well as those that are not. For example, the advisor may wish to prohibit discussions concerning current problems between the advisee and the advisee's immediate family. The agreement that is negotiated, then, would contain a stipulation that the advisor is unwilling to take part in discussions that are so focused.

There are other reasons for formulating the advising contract in the early stages of the relationship between advisor and advisee. According to Erving Goffman, "An individual can more easily make a choice as to what line of treatment to demand from and extend to others present at the beginning of an encounter than he can alter the line of treatment that is being pursued once the interaction is under way."[10] For both advisor and advisee, the time to set the conditions of the advising interaction is during the initial contact. Early shared agreements help avoid the solidifications of advisor-advisee interaction that result from unspoken expectations, assumptions, and early precedent-setting interchange between advisor and advisee.

What to Include in the Contract

A contract is defined in Webster's as "an agreement between two or more persons to do or forbear something; a bargain; or a covenant." Now the term *forbear* may also mean "to endure," which, for some aspects of advising, seems fairly descriptive. For our purpose, the advising contract is the result of a deliberate public process between advisor and advisee that entails describing the tasks to be undertaken and the responsibilities of each party. The nature of the agreement will certainly vary from one advisor to another and may even be different between one advisor and each of a number of advisees. In each case, however, the contract represents a product of preliminary discussions between advisor and advisee regarding the nature of the process they will share. The contract, then, should spell out the boundaries or limits of their advising relationship.

It seems that discussion leading to formulation of the advising contract would cover some of the following topics:

1. What expectations do advisor and advisee hold of each other and for advising?
2. What are the goals and objectives of advising?
3. What are the needs and resources of advisor and advisee?
4. How will they differentiate between advisor as technical-information assistant and advisor as adult?
5. How will they evaluate the advising relationship?
6. How will they handle difficulties (personal, interpersonal, or other) that arise?
7. How will they gather needed information?

The understandings reached between advisor and advisee serve to map the boundaries of the advising responsibilities of both parties. In the process, the understandings become the boundary of the advising process itself. Figure 8 illustrates how the individual responsibilities of both advisee and advisor in the advising process fall within the boundary of that set of activities, events, and procedures that both agree to call advising.

These three definitions of boundary make up the advising contract: (1) the specific tasks for which the advisor is responsible, (2) the responsibilities of the advisee, and (3) the definition of activities to be called advising.

Monitoring the Boundaries of the Contract

One important job for the advisor is to continually monitor the boundaries that have been established. Using the advising contract a means of understanding what activities or behaviors are agreed upon for both advisor and advisee and what subject matter, discussions, or work are appropriate, the advisor must be alert for signs that the boundaries, and thus the advising contract, are being breached or amended during the process of advising.

If, for instance, the contract called for the advisor to avoid specific action recommendations (i.e., "Why don't you take Bio 101 this term?"), requests for

FIGURE 8

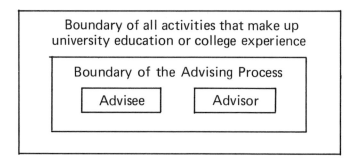

such responses by the advisee may be cause for reviewing the conditions of the agreement and pursuing a perhaps more basic question (i.e., "What makes it difficult for you—the advisee—to reach a decision on this matter?").

One of the advantages of constantly monitoring advising boundaries is that the responsibilities of each party for advising may be checked often. If the initial advising contract called for certain tasks or duties to be performed, then attention to the process of advising and the boundaries of that process also facilitates early discovery of nonperformance of specific duties. Data obtained from such an early warning device may then be used to explore causes of nonperformance, alternatives to the agreed-upon tasks or duties, or renegotiation of the advising contract to take into account these developments.

Another value of monitoring boundaries is that the review and discussion of boundary limits create a structure for the interaction of advisor and advisee. This framework for the advising interaction provides a degree of certainty and security for participants. Knowledge in advance of what is and is not acceptable behavior frees both partners to focus on the achievements rather than the restrictions of the relationship. Knowledge of the boundaries allows participants to plunge into that work which is acceptable rather than worrying about those areas that are to be avoided. The presence of the structure provided by the boundaries, however limited either might be, serves to help participants deal constructively with what otherwise might be difficult and anxiety-producing situations. Boundaries, then, help partners in the advising process accomplish what they say they wish to accomplish.

KEEPING THE RELATIONSHIP ALIVE

One important responsibility of the advisor is to act as a "boundary patrol"—monitoring the progress or direction of the advising, as well as the adherence of both parties to the advising contract. Although it is possible for the advisee to perform some of these functions, the primary responsibility rests with the advisor. To perform such regulatory functions the advisor must seek, evaluate, and share information.

We are tempted to suggest that the monitoring activities are simply a matter of good communication between advisor and advisee. However, the maintenance of good, open communication is anything but simple. Attempts on your part to maintain or improve the level of communication between you and your advisee will require, beyond some minimal level of skill, some degree of personal courage. Data about advising communication is information about proficiencies in and consequences of activities for which you bear some measure of responsibility. Furthermore, that data may suggest that it is your deficiency that leads to poor understanding between yourself and your advisee. Therein lies the need for personal courage.

What seems to be appropriate for clarifying the communication aspect of advising? First, one needs to develop a way for collecting or generating data. Second, one needs to determine what potential areas are fruitful for collecting data. Third, one needs to think about the way in which the feedback is to be used to improve the situation.

Let's start at the beginning. How do we go about getting the data? A moment's thought will produce an answer—we do it by using face-to-face questions during the advising interchange. That doesn't sound hard—right? Well, if it doesn't, it should. Asking questions, appropriate questions to get a meaningful response, is a skill most of us simply don't possess unless we have had training. Such a training program is beyond the scope of this booklet, but it may be readily available elsewhere in your institution. In fact, we strongly recommend that if you are interested in developing this skill, useful in many aspects of life, you consult *The Art of Helping* and *The Art of Problem-Solving*, both by Robert R. Carkhuff.[11]

In a nutshell, we suggest that you follow one very simple guideline in formulating your questions so that they produce data: don't phrase questions so that they have double meanings or convey value judgments that preclude an honest answer (i.e., "You're not seriously thinking of dropping that course, are you?"). A question such as "Is that answer satisfactory?" does not produce the data that "What in my response troubles you?" might. Similarly, "Do you understand why you are required. . .?" will probably not be as productive as "What further questions do you have as a result of our discussion?" Questions that have yes or no answers usually don't help much. Questions that expand horizons usually do. Remember, too, that questions should be formulated in terms of the advising contract and your knowledge of the advisee's communication hierarchy: if you are both on the same communication level, judgmental and value-loaded questions can be successfully entertained.

What areas are appropriate and fruitful for data gathering, even if you feel the need to sharpen your questioning and listening skills? One very general area that may often be used pertains to the quality of the most recent advising interaction. Data relating to this may be generated by posing questions to your advisee and yourself. Questions such as "How do you feel about what we're doing?", "What are the benefits (consequences) of what we're doing?", "How well are we listening to each other?", "What are we trying to accomplish here?" are some that could be used. A public response to such general questions provides information about the degree of shared perception or feeling about the advising interaction. If differences are reported, a cooperative effort to determine possible sources of such differences may be undertaken. These general questions about the advising interaction may be raised at many points in the advising process. Each intervention of this type results in a check of the views of both parties and, if needed, initiates the process of moving from general to specific understandings.

Review of the Advising Contract

One type of understanding that requires periodic review is that pertaining to the advising contract. A review serves to contrast a general notion of what advising should accomplish with specific situations or needs that develop during the process. A comparison by advisor and advisee of the general advising contract and specific developments will permit deliberations about whether or not the agreement should be altered or the specific request overlooked. The point to be made is that such a review is not undertaken to allow either the advisor or the advisee to avoid dealing with some matter, but rather to ensure that they understand and agree on just what is to be undertaken. Even the definition of one key term may serve as an obstacle. For example, suppose advisor and advisee agree that "guidance for courses" is an appropriate matter to be dealt with in the advising interaction. If the advisor's understanding of the term is "description of course content" but the advisee's understanding is "how coursework contributes to career interest," the stage is set for confusion and disappointment unless the term "guidance for courses" is changed or defined more clearly.

The clarification of terms and the determination of specific duties and responsibilities of each participant are part of the activity of establishing and maintaining advising boundaries. The specifications of the advising contract provide definitions of advising that set advising apart from other activities that are part of the lives of advisor or advisee. Within the boundaries of advising, the advising contract also defines the responsibilities of advisor and advisee. Both advisor and advisee should often try to check the current level of shared understanding of what advising is to encompass, or the individual duties or responsibilities of either person. The goal of the advising relationship is preventive maintenance, not remedial restoration.

Using a Visual Model for Planning

One area that proves difficult during advising is the prediction or location of advisee needs; that is, of all the many topics that could be discussed, which are of a higher priority? What information is needed? By what date? For what purpose? What questions or issues need to be addressed? These are but a few of the questions that advisee and advisor must answer. One approach that may be used to generate data to answer such questions involves using a visual model for planning. Advisee and advisor may work together to build an actual and projected time line of the advisee's educational program. Included might be significant decision points such as deadlines for registration, key information needed, questions or issues to be confronted, alternatives to be examined, activities to be completed, and persons to be seen. The actual construction and periodic examination of the visual model may assist in identifying both the need and its

Figure 9

Visual Model for Terry Parsons, Freshman

1st meeting	2nd meeting	3rd meeting	4th meeting
Orientation week	major/minor	midterms	courses
regular courses	dorm life?	tutor?	next semester
registration	course progress	physics	physics?
services?			

5th meeting	6th meeting	7th meeting
first-term grades	summer job?	firm up sophomore plans
waive?	summer course?	campus job?
tutor for Physics III	Sophomore courses	
	housing	

1st meeting Sophomore year	2nd meeting	3rd meeting	4th meeting
review first year	midterms	second-term courses?	review major
first-term courses	Biochemistry	Physics required	what minor?
problems?			first-term grades

5th meeting	6th meeting
requirement for major electives	summer plans?
	two-year progress
postgraduate notions	transfer to major advisor
	Talk with others in major

temporal position in the advisee's educational program. The visual model may also come in handy when discussing the advising contract and boundaries. The model serves as one reminder of what is to be done and when, and should contribute significantly to discussions of how, why, or by whom.

Figure 9 provides an illustration of a visual model produced by advisor and advisee. Creation of the visual model stimulates both parties to consider the issues or questions to be handled as well as the information or decisions that may be required. In addition, the model lends itself to determining when the items or questions can be scheduled for review or examination. One consequence of building and using a visual model is the recognition that the advising relationship is a process involving planning, change, and evaluation and not just a series of isolated events.

One last word about gathering data for the advising relationship. This discussion should not be interpreted as advocating that the advisor have sole responsibility for the gathering of information. It seems appropriate to us that the advising agreement should include discussion of the advisee's responsibility and resources for data gathering activities. Whether focused on the advising interaction or directed toward answering specific advising-related questions, data generating efforts on the part of the advisee are valuable additions to the advising process.

DIFFICULT TIMES: TIPS AND PROBLEMS

What we intend to do in this chapter is discuss these difficulties most likely to have a high prevalence among advisors. But the notion of describing any portion of the myriad of possibilities arising from the interaction of two bright and achievement-oriented persons does, indeed, give us pause. Drawing on a reservoir of projections and good intentions, rather than experience gained at the cutting edge of your advisor's chair, we push on.

Ineffective Communication and Risk-Taking

Ineffective communication (discussed in the preceding section) is perhaps the principal source of difficulty in advising. It seems that much of the tension and dismay that arises during advising could, in many cases, be alleviated or even prevented with thorough and continuing communication between advisor and advisee. "Why is this so?" you may ask. "If communication is so important, why does it occur so infrequently between persons?" Almost everyone probably has some explanation. We think communications are poor generally because (1) it does take time, (2) it involves taking risks in the form of seeking feedback, and (3) the feedback at times includes data you would rather not hear or do something about. One result is that many problems between advisor and advisee either stem from poor communication or are made more serious due to ineffective communication.

Situations revolving around a clash in personality or conflicting personal agendas of advisor and advisee, changing the advising contract, referral or the use of other resources, or even the problem of time constraints or unwieldy schedules are made much more cumbersome if the communication is ineffectual. Many of the situations mentioned, as well as a host of others you could provide, involve the recognition, acceptance, and resolution of conflict between persons. For most of us the presence, let alone the management, of conflict is unsettling. In this arena, the identification and management of conflict in the advising process, advisors may make major contributions.

This conclusion is based on a number of assumptions, first among them that advisees view the advisor as holding achieved status and, as a result, generally attribute high legitimate power or social esteem to the advisor. After all, the institution selected you over many others to fill the role of professor or researcher. Should this not also be true of your selection as advisor? The advisee, probably like so many of us for whom past experience with counselors or advisors may have been disappointing, is still hopeful that this advisor, this time, will be different. You are, at least until your advisee gains contrary data, perceived as a paragon of assistance.

A second assumption is that advisees expect or take for granted that advisors will perform competently as adults in their adult role. Furthermore, you may expect advisees to conclude that competent performance by you in the adult role is supereminent—that beyond your technical brilliance as faculty advisor you will be Renaissance Man or Mark Hopkins on the other end of the log.

Third, your failure in meeting expectations in the role of adult, as must happen to all of us, creates for the advisee a strong negative reaction toward you. The consequence of your not meeting the idealized versions of what adults could or should be punctures once again the advisee's search for the perfect model of what it means to be an adult.

Finally, management of conflict and issues surrounding the exercise of authority are pervasive developmental concerns that all of us must face. A

34

substantial part of the concerns of youth have to do with coping with conflict and dealing with authority. So, too, advisees, or at least a goodly number of them, seek resolutions to questions and feelings that arise from these two problem sources. It seems to us that a major value of having advisors incorporate the adult role in the advising process is to provide one highly visible and accessible adult role model for the advisee.

Consequently, it is important that the advisor take the lead—in actuality, provide the model for good communication—in voicing the difficult questions and in taking the risk of daring to be wrong by facing sensitive issues in the relationship between advisor and advisee. The fact that dealing with conflict or authority may touch a sensitive area does not imply that the advisor need assume roles of healer, counselor, or therapist. You are, after all, a partner in a task-oriented activity, a teacher and a person to be sure, but committed in this relationship only to advising. Your commitment to the advising task, however, may be the necessary but barely sufficient motivation for initiating those risky queries.

The "Fragile" Advisee

Another one of those difficult times is encountered in dealing with an advisee who appears psychologically "fragile" or overly dependent on the advisor. The expressed concern for the advisee is acutely felt by the advisor. The tortured ambivalence of what to do or say is familiar to many advisors. "Do I treat this one like my other advisees?" "Do I acknowledge my uncertainty?" "Should I suggest a different advisor as a solution?" "Should I do what I'm comfortable with and let the chips fall?"

The issue is complex and solutions uncertain. A beginning, however, is to check or review your perspective of the situation with a competent and trust-worthy third party. Another advisor, a member of the counseling or mental health service staff, your advising coordinator—all may prove helpful in assisting you in a review and in planning an appropriate course of action. Examination of the particular situation may suggest broaching the subject with the advisee, exploring alternative sources of assistance, and perhaps, initiating a referral to that source. Your consideration for the advisee and your action as one adult helping another go a long way in providing the advisee with the degree of support, encouragement, and reality-based action that is to be expected of the competent advisor.

Extremes of Verbal Competence

A third area of some difficulty is working with advisees who may be located at the extremes of a continuum of behavior labeled "arrogantly assertive" to "catatonically shy." In either case, the advisee is reluctant to have much to do with the advisor, although the reasons are certainly different. There may be, however, some not-so-obvious similarities. One may hypothesize that in both situations the advisee is finding it difficult to trust the advisor. For one type of advisee, the bluff and bravado may be only a different version of what another strives to accomplish through inactivity and silence—that is, protection of self, resistance to permitting the advisor to observe all of what he or she is or might become.

Although it is impossible to suggest advisor behavior that is guaranteed to work, one procedure may improve prospects for a better relationship between advisor and advisee. In this case, the advisor assumes responsibility for observing and then describing to the advisee the latter's behavior. Through description of advisee behavior, the advisor invites corroboration of perceptions and discussion of what factors prompt the behavior, what the behavior is designed to accomplish, and whether or not the advisee wishes to change the behavior. The advisor, although labeling and describing the behavior, accords respect to the advisee by acknowledging that the power to explain, discuss, or change the behavior rests with the advisee. This form of advisor behavior may be one step in the development of trust of the advisor by the advisee.

Objectives for Advising

One area related to your awareness of roles for advisors has the potential for creating difficulty. We speak here of your perception of appropriate functions for advising. What are the objectives of advising? . . . to respond to any advisee difficulty? . . . to be selective in attempting to provide assistance?

Depending upon your competence, interest, and schedule you may interpret advising as incorporating some combination of the following functions and objectives:

1. Academic advising refers to specific academic matters, such as, course selection, programming, dropping and adding courses, and advice rendered to your students concerning academic programs and careers.
2. Career advising is that form of academic advising that you do to translate career choices into educational goals and programs and to relate academic curricula to career opportunities.

Related but not integral to advising are the following functions:

1. Counseling or assisting students in dealing with emotional or psychological adjustment problems;
2. Career counseling using psychological procedures to help a student with the self-evaluation and recognition of capabilities and interests; and
3. Career planning relating the outcome of the evaluation of career counseling to information currently available about world of work.

Advising may be represented as a set of activities that are related to, but differentiated from, the activities of counseling, career counseling, and career planning. Figure 10 indicates possible relationships and overlapping functions between activities that cluster around the designation "advising." An ever-present difficulty is that of stating and then maintaining a conception of what you wish advising to be.

> The intent here is to establish as clearly as possible the authors' definitions and objectives. Our task is not to convince you of their validity but to communicate them as forthrightly as possible. This procedure, we believe, has merit for you and for your advisees also.

FIGURE 10

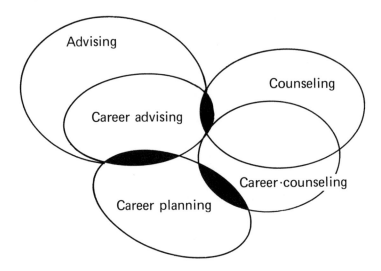

Your conclusion about objectives and functions for advising constitute the foundation of your involvement as an advisor. The challenge lies in the responsibility of making sure that you and your advisee are talking about the same process when you discuss advising.

Unequal Relationships

A development that may present some degree of difficulty occurs when the advisee, the advisor, or both experience a heightened attraction for the other. This personal magnetism increases the intensity and tension of the relationship. Although one may assume that some proportion of these developments are sexually oriented, there are certainly other bases for undue fascination with the other person.

For instance, the other person may remind one of a dearly loved relative or friend. Mannerisms or characteristics may be strikingly similar to one's child, sibling, or youthful relative, or, in the case of the advisee, one's parent, coach, or adult relative. Similarly, the other person may symbolize for one party the personification of the other role. Thus, for the advisee, the advisor may be viewed as the ideal adult while the advisor may view the advisee as the model adolescent.

Whatever the basis for the quickening of interest of one in the other, the relationship between them is subjected to additional pressures. The discussion so far may lead you to conclude that such personal attractions are unhealthy and should be avoided whenever possible. It is presumptuous, we believe, to predict that such "added attractions" will have either positive or negative influences. It is certainly conceivable that such attractions may do as much to benefit the relationship as they may do to detract from the relationship. We are not concerned with directionality of influence, but rather with the fact that a new and different pressure may be present in the relationship.

One result of this added pressure of strong interest by one party in the other is that roles and role expectations may be altered. Difficulty does not automatically result from a shift in role, but rather from changes in the mutual understanding of what roles are appropriate in the advising relationship. For instance, the shift by one party to perceiving the other as an attractive sexual partner may lead, to say the least, to some very confusing verbal exchanges during the advising interaction.

In the event of advisor interest in the advisee, an additional option is available. Although you may decide to discuss the situation with the advisee, an alternative is to discuss your perception of the matter with a trusted third party. In discussion with a third party—another advisor, colleague, or counselor—you can seek a better understanding of, and responses to, the factors involved in the relationship.

Right To Fail

The final problem area we wish to mention, although there are certainly many others you might wish to discuss, is that of respecting the advisee's right to fail.

In interaction with other adults, most of us probably feel comfortable in questioning, suggesting, advising, and warning, but respect the right of the other in reaching a decision and pursuing a course of action. Your approach to adults in this respect is also an appropriate response to your advisees. You can share your information and experience, verbalize recommendations and reservations, but in the end you must step aside to allow the advisee to do what she or he alone can do: make decisions and assume responsibility for them. Indications of the advisor's contribution might be reflected more in the fact that advisees exercise some control over their own lives and less on advisor interpretations of the quality of decisions made or type of life selected. The prospect of the advisee involved in the process of education and the advisor as an agent fostering educational progress of advisees requires no less stringent a measure than acceptance of responsibility by the advisee.

INFORMATIONAL ADVISING

The Bare Minimum

The most important thing to recognize about Level A, or informational, advising is that everyone—faculty, administrators, and students—agree that this is the minimum an advisor must provide. You must be knowledgeable about the requirements, policies, and procedures of the institution, and very likely you will be expected to be knowledgeable about courses, resources, and various student services or helping agencies on campus. Information is to advising what knowledge of the subject matter is to teaching: shortcomings in other aspects will be tolerated or excused, but a shortcoming in knowledge or content can be fatal. Clearly, if you have a limited amount of time to spend on advising skills, this is the place to spend it. If you are an adequate informational advisor, you will rarely be criticized; if you are not, there is little prospect that anyone will be satisfied with your effort. Because it is the one aspect of advising on which your performance may be judged, it is important to know how to approach this kind of advising and how to handle it well.

This is, of course, to view the matter from the top down. It is the view of the administrator, the department chairperson, the advising system manager; and, as much as we may wish to ignore or discount their views, it cannot be ignored in a practical sense. Your understanding and acceptance of this has important repercussions in negotiating your advising contract, for informational advising is the least that you will probably be able to settle for in agreeing to be an advisor.

But don't fall into the trap of thinking this is the only reason that informational advising is important. While it is certainly good to be cognizant of the expectations of students and administrators, these expectations are certainly not strong enough to insure adequate informational advising. Viewing the matter in that light would put an entirely negative motivation on informational advising, a motivation that hardly justifies including this aspect of advising for discussion here. There are many sound positive reasons for making sure you are an adequate informational advisor.

Information, Please

If you are an experienced advisor, you may well point out that informational advising is primarily important because 80 percent of advising is informational in nature: you spend most of your time answering often simple questions on a wide variety of topics, without any visible strings attached. Yet in discussing advising in this booklet we have talked about it in a very different way; we have emphasized an entirely different side of the activity, one that you may not have encountered in your experience as an advisor or may not consider very important. This may lead you to suspect that we are "all wet," that we haven't much experience in advising students, that we are biasing the discussion as social scientists rather than practitioners. This is hardly the case, for in our own view, we consider informational advising so important and so little understood that we think it deserves a chapter of its own.

Why do we consider informational advising so important? Because if you don't have command of basic information, you will *never* be able to establish an advising relationship with a student. At the outset, an advisee comes to you to ask some questions, and his or her opinion of you as an advisor will suffer if you don't have the answers. This is particularly true because the questions at the beginning of the relationship are almost always informational questions of a more or less trivial nature: freshmen want to know where the bookstore is, how they register, what books to buy, etc., but they rarely begin by asking a total stranger (you) about the basic issues of their lives. We need to recognize that all relationships start with a testing period, and, in advising, the testing period is one of easy, informational questions. If you fail here, you can forget any subsequent interaction, no matter how much you know about writing contracts, counseling, or the dynamics of personal relationships.

This little-recognized fact produces one of the real myths of advising. Ask a faculty member about advising, and almost all advisors will tell you that advising is basically answering very simple questions about regulations, procedures, and policies—and in the next breath they will tell you that the most discouraging fact about advising is that students never come in to see their advisor, never establish a meaningful relationship. They may, in fact, ask why this occurs. The explanation is simple: most faculty advisors fail to have an adequate command of essential information; they lose credibility with advisees during the first encounter, and thereafter the advisee goes elsewhere—preferably to the source who does have the information. One very serious shortcoming of many advisors is that they don't realize *why* informational advising is so important. If they understood the importance of information as a bridge builder to further interchanges, they would not wonder why students do not come back, and they would see informational advising in a different light.

Since the lack of information is the principal reason students do not return to their advisors, it is essential to know how you stand in this area. We believe the best way for you to determine that is by taking a short quiz; check your answers to the following questions with an authority at your institution to be sure the answer you give is correct.

1. What is the class profile of the entering class? That is, what is the average SAT, class rank, and so forth?
2. What percentage of the class receives financial aid? What is the average award? What kinds of financial aid packages are given?
3. What percentage of the freshman class "drops out"? What are the principal reasons? Is the number rising or falling?
4. What obstacles face students who wish to transfer between units? What grades are necessary? Do they lose a scholarship?
5. What are the current graduation requirements? What are the current requirements for good standing? Do you have a copy of faculty legislation regarding requirements?
6. What are the procedures for taking a leave of absence? Will students receive credit for work done on leave?
7. Who is responsible for counseling persons with severe emotional or psychological problems? Have you ever talked with him or her—enough so that you could take a student and introduce him or her without feeling awkward?
8. Who sets advising policy? Who determines the number of advisees you will have?
9. What is the thrust of the Buckley Amendment?

If you can answer all of these quickly and accurately, you know your stuff. If you can't, then you have some work to do. You are, whether you wish to admit it or not, lacking in essential information.

This leads to another very curious fact: a lack of information is probably the single greatest shortcoming in the largest number of advisors. It is curious because most advisors clearly recognize the importance of informational advising.

But if advisors recognize that informational advising is important, even if they don't understand why, what is behind their failure to master the essential information? One reason is that most of us *think* we know the information. After all, we work here, we serve on committees, we make the rules, and we have been here long enough to know what is going on. To admit ignorance is a difficult thing. Yet most of us are ignorant, much more so than we generally believe, and our unwillingness to admit this keeps us from learning essential information. That is why we included the foregoing quiz, and we hope you tried to answer the questions. In informational advising, the first step toward improvement is recognizing that simply being a part of an institution does not go very far toward guaranteeing that you know much about the general affairs affecting students.

There is another reason that advisors have generally failed to become knowledgeable about important information, and that is the rise of professional counselors, staff, or advisors as separate entities on campus. While they may be trained in counseling techniques, these professionals are often information specialists as well, often as much by necessity as by choice. One of the curious things is that these persons can often answer the questions on the above quiz better than anyone else. As an interesting sidelight, at some point you might enjoy giving the quiz to such a person and to one of your friends on the faculty for comparison. In any case, the advent of these generalists on campus relieved the faculty of the need to answer many of these questions. Since we don't need to answer the questions, we soon find that we are no longer knowledgeable in many of these areas.

The other factor that has affected our ability to answer questions is an information explosion on campus. Even when we are interested in keeping abreast, it has become impossible because of the expansion and specialization in the educational enterprise. Information proliferates far faster than we can keep track of it. Suppose, for example, you were interested in financial aid, since this affects so many students today. To be able to answer questions in this area, you would need periodic briefings by a specialist, primarily because local, state and federal governments have increased the ways in which aid is available, and institutions now require numerous forms, confidential statements, and tax returns to determine eligibility. We all realize that academic disciplines expand year after year, with more and more journals being published; we need also to realize that the information required to do successful advising has increased at an equally rapid rate.

We are now in a position to understand why informational advising is so important, and why most of us don't do a better job with this aspect of advising. What can be done to remedy this shortcoming?

What Do You Need To Know?

As an advisor, perhaps without experience, what information do you need to know? That is going to vary considerably from institution to institution, so the first thing you ought to do is go to the manager of the advising system and ask what you are expected to know. Usually the answer will be in the form of an *Advisors' Handbook* or some such thing; if it isn't, you will probably have to settle for a verbal definition, which may be rambling, indefinite, and not very helpful.

Since you may not know what you need to know until it is too late (many advising system managers feel the best way to learn is to let unprepared faculty "get their feet wet"), we have taken the liberty of providing a simple checklist. You should know *the who, the where,* and *the how* of the following subjects (i.e., *who* should a student see, *where* does he or she go to see him or her and how should he or she proceed):

1. Admissions, including the location of admissions folders, how they can be used to determine abilities of students, etc.;
2. Housing, including how students are paired with roommates, procedures for making a change, ways of financing;
3. Financial aid, including types of packages, policies of awarding, coordination of on-campus jobs, affect of grades upon;
4. Uniform voluntary separations, including leaves of absence, withdrawals, in-absentia study, internal transfer, external transfer;
5. Sources of academic assistance, including remedial courses, tutoring services, speed reading classes, study skills assistance;
6. Involuntary separations, including suspensions, re-admission after suspension, options during suspension, good standing, input to decision-maker;
7. Graduation requirements, including hours required, subject matter requirements, majors, minors, waiving requirements, advanced placement, transfer credit;
8. Course selection, including adding, dropping, substituting courses, preregistration procedures, late fees, final dates, making changes in schedule;
9. Personal counseling, including crisis counseling, sex counseling, drug counseling; and
10. Confidentiality, including the Buckley Amendment, who has access to information, to whom information may be disclosed safely.

By this time you are probably saying that you can't possibly understand all of these areas. You're right. But you need to know a minimal amount about each one, enough to be conversant in each area, so that you can be helpful even if you can't provide the answer yourself. The strategy is as important as the specific little bits of information. It is important to know your way around—and knowing your way around means being able to refer a student to the person who has the answer, not to the person who may know the person who has the answer.

How to Get the Information

Obviously the items we have mentioned cover a lot of information. You can't get a command of the information by doing the routine things we all do—even if it is for a period of time such as five years. Nor can you get the information by yourself, at least you can't do it very efficiently that way. The best way to become informed is to require the advising system manager to provide that function.

For example, when you work out your advising contract, agree that informational advising can be required of you only if there is a mechanism to give you the essential information. In short, be sure that the manager shares the responsibility for getting you the information essential to your success as an advisor.

The fly in the ointment here is likely to be the mechanism. We have already made mention of the fact that many institutions have an *Advisors' Handbook* reputed to contain the necessary information. Some of the publications are quite good, others are quite bad. If this is the mechanism offered to you, ask to read it over before you rate this as acceptable. Check for brevity and clarity: does the book tell you what to do, or does it cite endless rules and regulations? Good handbooks are usually very brief, to the point, well indexed, and contain diagrams or other visual aids. Beware the ponderous handbook—it may well make things worse rather than better.

An alternative to the handbook is an orientation session for advisors, coupled with follow-up workshops. Such an arrangement has the advantage of letting you ask questions, opening up discussion regarding policy, and enabling you to learn from the experiences of other advisors. It also provides a format that can be expanded considerably in a variety of areas, depending upon the needs of the group. Some advisors object to the time that is required for such workshops, and certainly every effort should be made to keep workshops short and to the point; most advisors find less time is spent in workshops than would be spent calling around trying to find the answer. Perhaps the old law about an ounce of prevention being more valuable than a pound of cure is applicable here. Our experiences would indicate the regularly scheduled advisors' workshops are an invaluable aid in preparing advisors for the task of informational advising.

A third means that is frequently applied is the "advising memo," and many advisors say they prefer this means over either of the other two. In negotiating with the advising system manager, you may want to discuss this alternative, which puts considerable pressure on the manager to produce timely, well-written memos. Most managers feel this system puts too much responsibility on them and too little on you, and you should expect some resistance on that account. Irrespective of these objections, it is our experience that advising memos are not very successful at getting the information across. Institutions suffer from their own brand of junk mail and this mimeo mania results in a callous indifference toward most mimeographed mail.

We recommend that if you are interested in being a good advisor, you try to negotiate all of these elements in your advising contract. The better the support program for you, the better you will be as an advisor. If there is no support program planned or available, you will not only be vulnerable, you will be forced to spend valuable time by inefficiently seeking the answers for yourself. Insist on a good support program if for no other reason than to make sure the manager realizes that advising is a two-way street, with both parties having significant obligations to each other. If you can make this point forcibly, you will have taken a great step toward making your job easier and more enjoyable.

We have discussed *what* advisors need to know and ways that they can get this information easily and accurately. The mechanism for ensuring support is negotiation: support through workshops, etc., is the price you should extract in return for agreeing that informational advising is the standard of acceptable advising performance.

MODELS FOR ADVISING

As a faculty advisor, you may frequently find yourself thinking that you know pretty much what you want to do, but that you are really not as successful as you would like to be in reaching desired outcomes. The difficulty usually lies in the fact that you have to use words to achieve your goal. The problems inherent in any conversation between two persons are myriad, and we don't pretend to be able to resolve them. What we offer for your consideration in this section are two model advising conversations (models in the sense that they can be used for instruction even though they in no way represent perfection). Think for a moment of the prospect of traveling in another country where you have little or no knowledge of the language. You might go to the campus bookstore and buy a short primer on the language, one that presents model conversations. Our models are, in a sense, very much like the conversations in a language book for tourists: that is, if you master them, these high-frequency interactions will serve to "get you by" most situations. As such, our models are a crutch for the beginner, and once you become more proficient in the "language," you should shed these early helpers and develop more sophisticated versions of your own. In fact, we are confident that after you are "in the country" for a while, your facility with the language will greatly increase and you will have little or no difficulty whatsoever.

Lest our analogy be taken too literally, one proviso needs to be made. In advising, there is no distinct right or wrong way to construct a conversation. We offer *a* correct conversation. But there are other possibilities, just as there are numerous ways for a tourist to say "How much is that?" We can visualize every conversation as a branching system, as illustrated in Figure 11, with each response producing a series of optional responses. We cannot describe the entire tree, but we can easily describe one branch or route or subset of the whole. These are our models. Use them, try them on for size, modify them as the need arises. But don't forget, the other branches or possibilities are there, too, and you may wish to explore them as well.

Model 1

The Advising Contract: Negotiating with your Manager

This basic conversation assumes you have called, recognized your appointment as an advisor, and asked to discuss advising with your manager (see the Introduction). After the usual amenities, you initiate the discussion.

Advisor: What do you expect from advisors?

Manager: Oh, the usual kind of things. Help the freshmen get settled, select their courses, get them a tutor if they have trouble later on. I'm sure you've done most of it before.

A: Yes, you're probably right, but I'd like to be as specific as possible so that I can arrange my time to provide the service you expect. I'm teaching several classes, and I feel I have a heavy load, so that it might be best for both of us if we can come to a clear understanding now and avoid questions later on. Maybe I can ask specific questions and you can respond.

M: That sounds reasonable enough. But I'm still not sure all this is necessary.

FIGURE 11

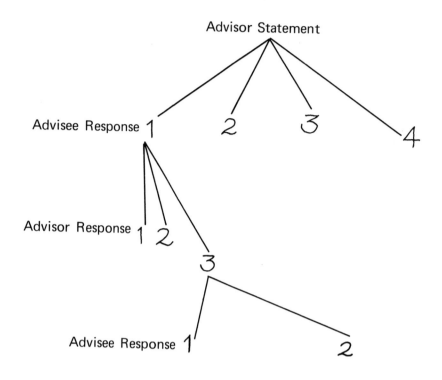

A: Will I be *evaluated* as an advisor?

M: Yes. You'll be evaluated via a survey given to your advisees.

A: What will I be evaluated on?

M: You'll be *evaluated on* availability, knowledge of courses, knowledge of
     procedures and policies, ability to refer students to correct resources,
     information on vocational and career plans, concern for academic
     progress, respect for decisions, and your understanding of personal
     needs. Quite frankly, I expect you to do a reasonable job on all these
     items. However, there is a *bare minimum of performance* that I insist
     on. You must post and keep office hours. You should know our basic
     courses well, you should be able to field any question on procedures
     and policies, and you should be able to refer students, because we will
     provide you with specific items of information on these areas. In my

view, it is your responsibility to attend all the advisors' workshops, where this information is communicated. Since the information is available, there is no excuse for ignorance. I also feel it is your responsibility to notify us when you are away from campus for extended periods, and to provide a replacement for your advisees during these times.

A: Will this evaluation be confidential and for my use or part of the record?

M: The returns will be confidential, primarily for your use in improving your performance, and will not be communicated to anyone else without your permission.

A: You indicated you believe the items you mentioned are a bare minimum, and I guess I agree that those are reasonable expectations. But you didn't mention *specific times* that I must be on campus for particular advising functions; is it safe to assume there are such times?

M: You have a good point. There are some times when we want you to be here. You should plan to be here for Orientation Week, for preregistration, for midterm grades, and for academic actions at the end of the term. I guess I would include your presence at these times as a "bare minimum."

A: I haven't given it a lot of thought, but I guess we can agree on your idea that there is certain information that I must know, and there are certain meetings I must attend, and certain times I must be here to fulfill specific functions. I hope, however, that these basics, including a description of what you expect for each function, will be given to us at a later date.

M: That seems fair enough. I'll be sure to write them down for all advisors. Are there any other questions?

A: Yes, there are. In my experience, there is a grey area of service that we haven't scratched yet. I'm wondering how much *responsibility* I have for my advisees' welfare. For example, if midterm grades are not good, should I call or wait for them to come in? Or when a student wants to drop a course, should I sign and give my approval, even if I'm not convinced? Do students have an absolute right to drop a course?

M: Those are good questions. Unfortunately, I don't have any pat answers.

A: It seems to me you have an obligation to provide answers to those questions.

M: I guess I agree with you to a certain extent. But I don't believe I have an obligation to provide definite answers, because I don't want to dictate a specific answer for all advisors, since this would negate a lot of creativity and freedom. I do agree that I have an obligation to provide a forum where advisors can discuss such questions and to provide access to experienced resources. Perhaps we should name an advising coordinator. Do you have another idea?

A: My inclination would be to have these questions discussed as part of the advisors' workshops or perhaps to provide a brown-bag lunch series. I'm not sure what the answer is, but I strongly feel that you have an obligation to provide that kind of support.

M: O.K. I'll accept that, though I want to give more thought to the actual arrangements.

A: Fine. Could we also talk about the *number* of advisees I will have? I tend to think you have an obligation to keep this group to a manageable size. I'm also anxious about how they are assigned.

M: Assignment is made on basis of field interest. I certainly would like to keep the number small, but I have only so many advisors for our entering students. I guess I would want to know what you think a manageable size is.

A: Fifteen seems a reasonable number.

M: I'm sorry, there's just no way you'll have only 15. It looks to me like it will probably be twice that number.

A: That's too many. Could we land in between? Say 20—perhaps 25 in a crunch.

M: I think I may be able to get it down to 22 or 23. I guess we can say that we can agree on 23. Or if that is impossible, I'll let you know in advance so that you can propose some alternatives. I think, however, that 23 is a very reasonable number.

A: Could we also agree on a mutually effective *way of registering complaints* about performance? I can envision that I may be dissatisfied with your support at some point or you might be dissatisfied with my advising, so I'd like to agree on a way to handle that.

M: That seems fairly easy to me, since I think we can treat each other responsibly. If I have a gripe, I'll grab the phone and give you a call, and you should feel free to do the same. The only stipulation I would want to add is that we talk to each other first, rather than mentioning anything to a third party. I wouldn't appreciate hearing from the Dean that you were dissatisfied, and I'm sure you wouldn't like to hear it that way either.

A: That's fair enough. I guess I have only one last point. How does the *college view advising?* Is that activity equal to teaching? If I advise, do I teach fewer students? What's the situation?

M: I view advising as part of every faculty member's responsibility. I don't believe in reducing teaching loads for advising, nor do I believe in letting any faculty member "escape" advising. I certainly would *not* pay for this activity. While I don't believe there is consensus regarding advising and promotion, I do like to take advising into consideration in salary adjustments. If this is a concern of others, perhaps we could discuss it at a departmental meeting. I'm afraid I can't give more of an answer than that.

A: O.K. I'm not satisfied with that, but if that's all there is at the moment, then I won't say any more now. I would like to see the issue discussed. I am concerned and I would like to do a good job.

M: Fine. I'll put it on the agenda. I think we've had a good discussion and I hope you will give me a call as other things pop up.

A: Don't worry, I will. I'm sure I haven't thought of everything, so let's leave it that *I will call* when other items come to mind. Thanks for spending your time. You've clarified a number of issues and that's been helpful.

In our model, the advisor initiates a focused discussion that covers:

1. Manager expectations of advising
2. Evaluation procedures and criteria
3. Performance criteria
4. Advisor on-campus availability
5. Responsibility of advisor for advisee
6. Responsibility of manager for advising
7. Number of advisees
8. Means of giving and receiving feedback about advising
9. Position of college on advising
10. Statement of topics requiring more discussion
11. Responsibility of advisor to contact manager.

The advisor leaves the meeting with knowledge about manager, department, and college perspectives on advising function, requirements, and procedures. The advisor is now aware of minimal standards to be met and has an understanding with the manager about continuing issues or questions and how these topics may be resolved.

Model 2

The First Meeting: Getting to know your advisee and laying the groundwork

Assume for the sake of simplicity that this meeting has been arranged by administrative staff and that the relationship is assigned (i.e., that the advisee knows you have not mutually selected one another and that he has never heard from you). The key concept in this conversation is that the advisor has the responsibility for taking the initiative and developing the contact. Initiative on the part of the advisee is a goal, not an accomplished fact.

Advisor: Hello, Terry, how are you? A little tired and confused at this point, I imagine.

Student: Yes, I guess that's pretty close to the truth. How are you?

A: Fine. Perhaps a little confused myself, but not very much. I'll tell you what I'd *like to do* while we have a few minutes together, and then you can *add some items* that you'd like to talk about. I'd like to tell you a little about myself, have you tell me a little about yourself, and then discuss what I think an advisor can provide, and what you think an advisor should provide. Does that sound reasonable? Anything you want to add?

S: Sounds all right to me. I can't think of anything to add right now.

A: Well, you probably will once we get going, so feel free to speak up. I'm thirty; I have three children, two boys and a girl, and I've been with the college four years. I guess I'm seen as a specialist in a particular field, but I think my work has a lot of other dimensions. I like to fish and golf, and attend most of the athletic events, concerts, and plays on campus. Most people would also say I'm a little nuts about tropical fish, since I have twenty tanks in my basement. I hope that you're a little crazy about something, too, so that you understand that part of my life. Let's find out about you. Tell me, why did you *select this college* and what do you do in the way of *outside interests*?

S: Well, I applied to a lot of schools, because I didn't know exactly what I wanted to do or who would accept me. I came here because I like the campus, the school has a good reputation, and it was a chance to get away from home a little bit. I guess my parents were anxious for me to come here, too, but they really didn't tell me where I should go.

I don't do anything very exciting. I did work as a camp counselor this past summer, which was a lot of fun. I really like swimming and hiking, and I had a chance to read some really good books.

A: That sounds great. Where was the camp? What sort of children were there?

> The advisor should pick up on some item about the advisee and pursue it so that the student realizes the advisor is interested in learning about him or her. Moreover, this will provide mental cues to help you remember your advisees next time.

A: Could we talk for a minute about advising? As you know, the college has assigned me as your advisor. That gives me a lot of freedom; I'd like to use that freedom by *coming to an agreement with you* about what we will do together. I personally feel that I am *most competent* to deal with academic affairs, especially the selection of courses and the procedures of the college. I'm probably a little *less competent* to deal with academic difficulties, though I do have experience on my side, and I feel a little uncomfortable with career or vocational planning when you get outside my field. I'd like to discuss a philosophy of planning, however, and share my thoughts on what kinds of considerations have value. *How do you feel* about what I've said so far?

S: I guess I'm still wondering what advising is supposed to do for me.

A: I'd be very happy to talk about that. Perhaps I can help you out by being more specific. Our *first task* will be to select a schedule of courses, and I'll help you there. But the next thing we'll face is the first round of examinations. I'd *prefer* that you drop by to tell me how you did, but if I don't hear from you, *I will call* to find out how you fared. Is that O.K.?

S: Sure.

A: Shortly after that, you'll need to preregister for the coming term, and I'd like you to come by to make an appointment. At that time, we'll review college graduation requirements, and talk about the various directions that your interests seem to be taking. I'd like at that time to tentatively plan a year ahead. I want you to give some thought to your *long-range goals* before you come. During our discussion we'll also talk about any difficulty you may be having. If you're not prepared, I'll ask you to come back later.

S: That doesn't sound quite fair. I'm not sure I can do all those things. I thought you were going to advise me. You make it sound like I have to make all the decisions on my own.

A: I'm glad you mentioned your feelings about what advising will require. This is the point we're trying to agree on, and I don't think we're very far apart. In essence, I will provide you with pertinent information for this process, but you have to provide input, too. I'm willing to help you clarify issues, values, and ideas, but I can't select for you. If you can make some basic decisions, I can help you implement them. I won't leave you high and dry, but *I won't do* all the work either.

S: That sounds more like what I expected. But I hope you call ahead of time if you want specific insights from me. I'm still a little hazy.

A: O.K., I'll either call in advance or be more specific when we meet again. I'd like to see you again shortly before final exams begin, primarily to find out how you stand, to discuss your progress over the past term, and to set out and review plans for advising for the next term. At that time, we can again decide who provides what in terms of the advising relationship for next term.

S: I have no objection to that. You've been very specific about our meetings, and I wonder if that means I won't see you any other time.

A: Not at all. Feel free to *come any time,* if you feel the need, though I prefer that you make an appointment to see me during office hours. If you really need me, you can call me at home. My number is 289-6738.

S: You've also mentioned mostly academic things, but I'm wondering about the possibilities of intramurals, particularly swimming.

A: I'm sure the availability of swimming is no problem, but you seem to be raising an issue about the *bounds of advising,* whether it extends beyond the academic. Is that part of what you are saying, or am I misinterpreting your question?

S: No, I guess that is part of my question.

A: This is a hard area for me, because in some areas outside of academics, I feel a little uncomfortable. Let's say that if it involves the kinds of things you have mentioned, such as swimming, club activities, etc., I certainly hope that you would drop in to see me. I'd also like to have you come in and rap about philosophy if you feel the need. Developmental problems are a little different though. I would like to share my experiences and ideas with you, but I really don't have sufficient knowledge to help much if serious developmental problems arise. I would want to refer you in that instance.

50

S: I don't think I follow you. You seem to be saying come in anytime—but don't come in for real problems.

I guess I'm a little confused by this. I've never really thought very much about what I expected of an advisor. Most of the time I just talk to my parents or my friends. I called my parents last night, but I can see that they don't know some of these things. I don't know anything at all about courses or rules, so I sure could use help there. Other than that, I had thought possibly about medicine, but I'm still pretty undecided. I hope we can talk about that sometime.

A: No, that's not what I am trying to say. What I am saying is that I would • want to share my values, experiences, and ideas, but that I am not competent to deal with severe personal problems that require specialized knowledge. Let's put it this way, in the academic area I'm an expert of sorts in terms of content, in the developmental area I am not an expert of content, but I do have a feel for the process since I have been through it. I'd be willing to share my experience, but I'm no great shakes as a diagnostician. I do want to emphasize one thing: I am not excluding personal questions from the advising relationship.

S: That makes things a little clearer. I guess I would say that I probably wouldn't want to include personal things, at least right now. For the time being, could we make it a more academically oriented relationship?

A: Certainly. So long as we agree to re-evaluate it later on. As the term rolls on, you may want to talk about some other things. For the time being, however, we can keep along the academic mainstream.

S: There is one other thing: do you have to *approve* all my courses?

A: I guess the answer is yes. But I wonder if you're also referring to a conflict between my role as an *authority* of the college and your *advocate*. Frankly, this is a difficult area. My position is that I am your advocate, that I will take up your cause within the university, that I will help you if you have conflicts with various rules and requirements. There is one restriction, however: you have to convince me of the justice of your cause. I will not support you simply because you say, I want to do this. You must convince me, as one adult to another, that there is merit in what you want to do. I will also make sure that you are aware of the rules and procedures and insist that you follow these until you convince me otherwise. In short, I won't assist you in subverting the rules, but I will support you when the cause is just.

S: Does that mean if I fail a course you'll bring it to the attention of the Dean?

A: No, not at all. That would hardly be supporting you. I simply won't give you a free ticket to do whatever you please. The relationship must have basic rules: *I'll support you if you act responsibly.*

S: That sounds fair enough. Will you call my parents if I do poorly?

A: No, not unless I speak to you first. I believe you should inform your parents, not me. So far as I am concerned, whatever we discuss *does not go beyond this room.*

Do you have any other questions?

S: No.

A: Can I sum up then to be sure we understand each other?

S: Sure.

A: O.K. *We agreed that . . . .*

During the first meeting the advisor was able to do the following:

1. Greet the student and acknowledge an awareness of the advisee's current experience.
2. Convey the notion of both advisor and advisee contributing to agenda for the meeting.
3. Share personal information about self.
4. Learn of advisee's reasons for selecting college and extracurricular interest.
5. Demonstrate advisor interest in student as person.
6. Identify for the advisee some particular competencies and deficiencies of advisor.
7. Enumerate some of the short- and long-range tasks for advising.
8. Identify requirements or responsibilities for advisee and advisor.
9. Specify availability of advisor.
10. Discuss appropriateness of topics for discussion within advising relationship.
11. Clarify advisor role regarding authority and advocate and advisor practice regarding confidentiality.

In addition, both advisor and advisee now know where each stands on matters of definition, objectives, and responsibilities regarding their roles in the advising process. The framework or shared understanding of what advising is, or may become, has been established and a genuine working agreement has resulted.

EPILOGUE

Following any activity one is tempted to ask, What has been accomplished? The question is as appropriate for the reader as it is for the writers.

Our goal has been to identify, describe, and discuss some aspects of the process of advising that are little discussed between advisors and colleagues, advisees, or supervisors. This presentation has been designed more to pose the question than fashion the answer. The answers, where they exist, are to be found in the interaction between you and your advisees.

This conclusion suggests another use for this booklet: as a discussion topic with your advisees. It seems to us that a critical analysis and discussion by you and your advisees of this booklet may serve the very purpose we hoped to achieve, that is, to facilitate the development of an interaction between advisor and advisee about the nature of advising. It is unimportant whether or not the discussion agrees or supports our definitions or conceptualizations. There may be many different approaches to understanding what advising is and how the process operates. What is important, however, is that you and your advisees develop a means of discussing, understanding, and using a model for advising that is mutually beneficial.

A related use of the booklet is that of facilitating discussions among advisors and with the manager. The booklet may lend itself to discussions about definitions of advising, requirements for advisors, needs of advisees, difficulties and problems encountered during advising, and tips on what to do next.

The last and, hopefully, most useful purpose served by the booklet is to provide you with some notions about advising. Along with provision of some seminal conceptions of the advising process, the booklet may serve as a stimulus to think through to your satisfaction what academic advising is, and means, in your professional work.

Advising, as we think of it here, can contribute to the major conditions for successful personal development during the college years mentioned by J. Katz:[12]

1. Facilitation of autonomy, of having a role in determining the situation and actions that affect one's life;
2. Opportunity to engage in actions that are useful to other people and useful to oneself;
3. Opportunity to produce work that results from the assertion or development of a competence and that is, to oneself, a satisfactory expression of oneself; and
4. Learning to act in concert with other people so that one's own perception becomes enhanced by being shared and developed with others and one's own capacities are developed through responsiveness to other people's needs and their responses to us.

Contributions made by your advising efforts will be remembered and appreciated for some years to come. Improvements at your end, therefore, may be associated with substantial outcomes for those whose lives you touch.

FOOTNOTES
AND
REFERENCES

FOOTNOTES AND REFERENCES

[1] Bazalgette, J. *Freedom, Authority, and the Young Adult.* New York: Pitman Publishing Corp., 1971.

[2] Chickering, Arthur W. *Education and Identity.* San Francisco: Jossey-Bass, 1969.

[3] Katz, J. "Psychodynamics of Development During the College Years." *Psychological Stress in the Campus Community.* (Edited by Bernard L. Bloom.) New York: Behavioral Publications, 1975. p. 45.

[4] *Ibid.,* p. 56.

[5] Bazalgette, J., *op. cit.*

[6] Bazalgette, J., *op. cit.,* p. 86.

[7] Rice, A.K. *The Modern University: A Model Organization.* London: Tavistock Publications, 1970. p. 61.

[8] Chickering, Arthur W., *op. cit.*

[9] King, Stanley H. *Five Lives at Harvard: Personality Change During College.* Cambridge, Mass.: Harvard University Press, 1973.

[10] Goffman, Erving. *The Presentation of Self in Everyday Life.* New York: Doubleday, 1959.

[11] Carkhuff, Robert R. *The Art of Helping: A Guide for Developing Helping Skills for Parents, Teachers, and Counselors.* Washington, D.C.: American Personnel and Guidance Association, 1973.

_____. *The Art of Problem-Solving.* Washington, D.C.: American Personnel and Guidance Association, 1972.

[12] Katz, J., *op. cit.,* p. 72.